Australian Aboriginal History

5 Stories of Indigenous Heroes

Marji Hill

**The Prison Tree Press
2021**

Copyright © 2021 Marji Hill
Copyright © 2018 Art work by Marji Hill 2018

Cover design: Marji Hill

First published as *First People Then and Now: Australian Aboriginal Heroes of the Resistance* by The Prison Tree Press, Gold Coast, Queensland, 2018.

ISBN: 978 0 9924118 6 2

 A catalogue record for this work is available from the National Library of Australia

All rights reserved. No part of this book may be reproduced, stored in a retrieval system, or transmitted in any form or by any means, electronic, mechanical, photocopying, recording, scanning, or otherwise,
without the prior written permission of the publisher.

Disclaimer

All the material contained in this book is provided for educational and informational purposes only. No responsibility can be taken for any results or outcomes resulting from the use of this material.

While every attempt has been made to provide information that is both accurate and effective, the author does not assume any responsibility for the accuracy or use/misuse of this information.

Aboriginal people are advised that this book contains the names of Aboriginal people who have passed away and that seeing their names may cause sadness and distress. The story of Aboriginal Australia could not be told without recognising their achievements.

The Prison Tree Press
Suite 124
1-10 Albert Avenue
Broadbeach, Queensland 4218
Australia

ACKNOWLEDGEMENTS

In the spirit of reconciliation, the author wishes to acknowledge the ancestral spirits and the traditional owners on whose land she lives, works and travels through.

Also, in the spirit of reconciliation the author's mission is to increase understanding between Aboriginal and Non-Aboriginal Australians and to provide people from all over the globe with some basic understanding of Australia's Aboriginal history and cultures.

I would like to thank Gwenyth Anthony and Virginia Frost for reading the manuscript and offering constructive feedback. I would also like to thank Eddie Dowd for his editing and preparing the manuscript for publication.

Marji Hill

Contents

1. Aboriginal Wars of Resistance 1
2. Pemulwuy 26
3. Musquito 35
4. Windradyne 42
5. Yagan 61
6. Jandamarra 90

Author & Artist 109

More Books by Marji Hill 113

Chapter 1

Aboriginal Wars of Resistance

Australian Aboriginal History

From 1788 for the next one hundred years casualties for Aboriginal people in northern Australia above the Tropic of Capricorn were well above 10,000. This was twice the number of those Non-Aboriginal Australians killed between the Boer War and the Vietnam War says Henry Reynolds in his book *The Other Side of the Frontier*.

The estimate is that 20,000 Aboriginal people died on Australian soil in defence of their country.

Violent conflict on the Australian frontier started on this continent soon after the arrival of the First Fleet in 1788. From this time on, Australia experienced constant warfare on its frontier. This continued right up to the early 1900s with the last massacre of the first people being recorded in 1928.

Australian Aboriginal History

The seeds of war were sown when it became clear that the British were taking over the continent and were going to occupy the lands belonging to Australia's Aboriginal people.

Initially, Aboriginal people who fought in defence of their country greatly underestimated the power of European firearms. Their experience was bloody when they realised that the musket was more powerful than any spear, boomerang, club or other weapon that they had ever devised.

But the success of Aboriginal resistance lay in their knowledge of their country, their lands, their food and water supplies, their skill in their traditional medicine and their ability to employ guerrilla tactics. Aboriginal resistance fighters could strike and then mysteriously melt away into the fastness of the Australian bush.

Their greatest successes were achieved with small guerrilla units operating at night in well planned attacks that were executed before dawn.

In defence of their country, Aboriginal resistance fighters used economic warfare as well as guerrilla tactics. They attacked and destroyed the property of the invaders. Sheep were speared or they were run into swamps or driven off cliffs; cattle were stampeded or injured, and horses slain.

Economic warfare was an effective defence that the Aboriginal resistance fighters had at their disposal.

1770

On 19 April 1770 Captain James Cook reached the east coast of Australia. His instructions were to take the eastern half of the continent for the British crown.

At Possession Island, off Cape York Peninsula in North Queensland, Cook took possession of the whole of the eastern coast in the name of King George III. Cook declared that Australia was *terra nullius*. This meant that Australia was a land without people and that it was unoccupied and unowned. Therefore, the belief of the time was that the English could justify claiming the continent of Australia as theirs.

Prior to 1788

Prior to 1788, the year that the First Fleet arrived from England, there were people from other countries who visited what was regarded as that "strange and unknown continent".

When the first visitors came is not known. For thousands of years there had been contact with the people of Papua New Guinea. When the sea levels were low the two countries – Papua New Guinea and Australia – were connected by land.

This was during the Ice Age. The people of Papua New Guinea, those of the Torres Strait and Cape York intermarried and exchanged cultural values, technology and survival techniques.

The Chinese admiral Ch'eng Ho ventured into uncharted waters bordering the Indian Ocean, including East Africa, India, Java and Sumatra. There has been some speculation that he may even have sailed into Australian waters between 1405 and 1432 on his great voyages of discovery.

Australian Aboriginal History

Macassans

Macassan fishermen from the Indonesian island of Sulewesi visited northern Australian shores. For several centuries until just after the end of the nineteenth century at least a thousand of them came to fish for the sea slug called trepang - a prized delicacy in Chinese cuisine.

The Macassans came every year. They stayed in northern Australia for approximately five months at a time before heading back to their own country.

The Macassans set up settlements on sheltered beaches along the coast of Arnhem Land in the Northern Territory. They built processing plants for treating the trepang. These consisted of rows of stone fireplaces which supported cauldrons in which the sea slug was boiled.

The second stage of the processing involved burying the trepang in the sand. It was smoked and then packed ready to be taken back to Macassar and the markets in Asia.

The Macassans interacted with the local Aboriginal people. Today, there are some people in Arnhem Land who have Macassan ancestors and relations. Some even travelled back to Macassar.

In 1907 the Australian government put an end to these visits by the Macassans because they had become a threat to the pearling industry.

The Portuguese and Spanish

In the sixteenth and seventeenth centuries Portuguese and Spanish navigators sailed the oceans near Australia. In 1605 the Spanish navigator, Pedro

Fernandes de Queirós claimed Vanuatu thinking it was the great southern land, and Luis Vaez de Torres in 1606 sailed through the waters that now bear his name – the Torres Strait.

The Dutch

In that same year 1606 the Dutch navigated the oceans around the northern, western and southern coasts. There were some unfriendly encounters with Aboriginal people which put them off from venturing further and exploring inland. In 1697 Willem de Vlamingh made an attempt at exploration but he also retreated.

Australian Aboriginal History

The French

Between 1771 and 1828 the French sent eight expeditions to Australia to extend their knowledge of the little known world of Australia and the Pacific. Many places in Australia are named after the French explorers: La Perouse, D'Entrecasteaux Channel, Freycinet, to name just a few.

The British

The arrival of the First Fleet from England in 1788 changed the course of history for Aborigines in Australia forever.

Given the concept of *terra nullius* - a land without people; a country that was unoccupied, and unowned - Captain Cook took the east coast of Australia and he named it "New Whales " then "New Wales". He finally settled on New South Wales. From this time on the Aboriginal inhabitants became a shadow people with no rights of any kind.

What the English did not know or acknowledge was that Australia, with its first people, was one of the earliest centres of civilisation in the world with its beginnings at least 65,000 years ago.

In some parts of the world invaders of countries attempted to or were forced to make agreements that at least partially recognised the rights of those people who had been occupied.

In 1840 in New Zealand there was the Treaty of Waitangi. Maori chiefs had full inclusive and undisturbed possession of their lands. In the United States and Canada, treaties were signed after long protracted wars with American and Canadian Indians.

Australian Aboriginal History

The legal fiction that Australia was unoccupied led to frontier wars on the Australian continent that lasted well over 100 years. A tragic and catastrophic history unfolded with the arrival of the First Fleet from England in 1788. This changed the course of history for Australia's first people forever.

First wars of resistance

Wars of resistance began in Sydney in the 1790s, and it was the people known as the Eora who were the first of the Aboriginal nations to defend their lands.

On 10 December 1790 an Aboriginal guerrilla leader got a notation in Governor Arthur Phillip's dispatches. This was Pemulwuy and for the next twelve years he led the resistance against the New South Wales Corps in the Sydney region.

Not only the Eora, but the neighbouring Dharuk people fought for their lands.

Another resistance fighter emerged in the Hawkesbury River area. His name was Musquito. He led many of the attacks on the colonists and their property along the New South Wales Central coast.

Dispossession and almost genocide characterised the occupation of the Australian continent for the next one hundred years. As white settlement spread throughout the country, para-military forces such as the Native Mounted Police were set up by the British to combat the resistance.

Fighting moved over the Great Dividing Range with the crossing of the Blue Mountains in 1813. Following the example of the Eora in Sydney, the Wiradjuri challenged the British presence for many long and terrible months. One of their resistance fighters, Windradyne, emerged as a leader of his people.

By the late 1830s the British intruded into the lands of the Kamilaroi who were pushed from their water supplies and robbed of their game.

1838 saw the massacre of Aboriginal men, women and children at Myall Creek and by the end of the 1830s the resistance wars stretched from northern New South Wales to western Victoria.

The Black War

The "Black War" (1824-31) began in earnest between Tasmanian Aborigines and the European trespassers. It was extremely violent and resulted in the near genocide of the Tasmanian Aboriginal population.

Australian Aboriginal History

The seeds of the Black War started in 1804 when Risdom Cove was occupied. The British had fired at the Aboriginal group who had come to protest against the aliens who were taking their food and occupying their country. At least three Aboriginal people were killed.

Settlers claimed lands in Tasmania and drove the Indigenous inhabitants away, murdering many. The Aboriginal warriors retaliated and killed settlers and their families, raiding houses and farms for food and resources, and trying to drive out the British.

In Tasmania the frontier war was intense and violent with the British invasion of traditional lands being the primary cause. Thousands and thousands of sheep had been driven onto traditional lands destroying centuries old ecosystems and upsetting food and water supplies.

Australian Aboriginal History

The British drove the Aboriginal inhabitants from their country killing many in the process.

By 1830 most of southeast Tasmania had been occupied by the non-Indigenous settlers who, in the eyes of the original people, were invading their lands.

Aboriginal resistance fighters armed only with spears and clubs, put up a strong and powerful opposition. They retaliated by killing settlers and raiding properties doing everything they could to drive out the alien forces.

In 1830 the Lieutenant-Governor of Tasmania, George Arthur, formed the "Black Line" which was a human chain that crossed the settled districts of Tasmania. His plan was to round up and capture the remaining Aboriginal people still living in the settled areas and drive them out.

Australian Aboriginal History

More than 2,000 soldiers, police and English formed the long Black Line across the north of the settled area from the coast to the southwest of Launceston. For thirty days they marched south aiming to drive the Aboriginal people to the Tasman Peninsula but in the end the Black Line failed.

The Black War was brought to a conclusion by George Robinson, the Tasmanian Protector of Aborigines. He negotiated with Aboriginal communities and persuaded them to give themselves up to be resettled.

By 1834 the remnants of the Aboriginal people in Tasmania had been relocated to Flinders Island in the Bass Strait.

One of these was the heroic and tragic Trugannini of the Tasmanian resistance. She had witnessed the invasion of her country and had seen the murder, kidnap and abuse of her family members.

While she was believed to be the last Tasmanian when she died in 1876 there are many Tasmanians of Aboriginal descent who continue their fight for rights today.

Resistance moves north

In 1824 in Queensland the first military post and prison was established in Moreton Bay. Aboriginal resistance started then and continued to the end of the century.

1845 saw the emergence of a powerful resistance leader in Dundalli (c.1820-1855). For many years Dundalli led the resistance in this region to drive out the intruders until he was eventually hanged in Brisbane.

It was legendary that Dundalli eluded capture for some fourteen years. The British tried to connect him with almost every act of violence and aggression committed in the region particularly on the northern side of the Brisbane River.

Queensland Aboriginal resistance moved north as time marched on throughout the 1800s. From 1857 to 1870 Aboriginal people fought in defence of their country in the Dawson River area.

There was resistance fighting in the Mackay and Bowen districts. In the 1880s it moved into the Cardwell district on the Palmer River and on to the Atherton Tablelands.

For ten years the Kalkadoons fought for their country in the Mount Isa and Cloncurry region culminating in the battle that took place at Battle Mountain in 1884.

Loaded guns hung in every room of every property homestead in Queensland and in the Northern Territory until the turn of the century.

The west

Resistance wars continued out from the east and south to all parts of the Australian continent.

In Western Australia when hostilities broke out with the British, another resistance hero emerged. This was Yagan who became a war leader in the tradition established by Pemulwuy.

Australian Aboriginal History

Yagan's story is about the invasion of Nyungar lands in the west by the British and how Aboriginal people fiercely defended their rights and their lands.

In the 1890s another resistance leader, Jandamarra, defended Bunuba lands. He led the insurrection against the British invaders in the Kimberley region in the far north of Western Australia.

Before the invasion by the British, Aborigines of Australia had defined territories and knew the boundaries of their traditional lands. They knew its physical features, its geography, animals, birds, fish and plants. They looked after their lands and ritually cared for their country with ceremony, songs, stories and art.

But with the invasion and the taking over of traditional lands for farming, precious Aboriginal cultures were almost destroyed. They fought to defend their country from the north to the south and from the east to the west. Not one State in Australia was immune from the resistance wars.

Aboriginal people of eastern Australia bore the full brunt of the British occupation of their lands and it was they who were the first to experience the dispossession of their culture. What took place in eastern Australia was repeated throughout the continent in Victoria, Tasmania, South Australia, West Australia, the Northern Territory and Queensland. There was no discussion with Aboriginal people, no treaty, and tragedy continued to unfold.

Pemulwuy, Musquito, Windradyne, Yagan and Jandamarra are just five Aboriginal resistance heroes, among many others, who fought and who stood up against the colonial occupiers of the Australian continent.

Here are their stories.

Australian Aboriginal History

Sources:

Australian Dictionary Of Biography. http://adb.anu.edu.au/biography/dundalli-12895

Barlow, Alex and Hill, Marji The Macmillan Encyclopedia Australia's Aboriginal Peoples. South Yarra, Vic., Macmillan Education, 2000.

Clements, Nicholas "Tasmania's Black War: a tragic case of lest we remember?" https://theconversation.com/tasmanias-black-war-a-tragic-case-of-lest-we-remember-25663 2014.

Grassby, Al and Hill, Marji Six Australian Battlefields: The Black Resistance To Invasion And The White Struggle Against Colonial Oppression. North Ryde, NSW , Angus & Robertson, 1988.

Hill, Marji First People Then And Now: Introducing Indigenous Australians. Gold Coast, Qld, The Prison Tree Press, 2017.

Reynolds, Henry The Other Side Of The Frontier. Townsville, History Department James Cook University, 1981.

Chapter 2

Pemulwuy
(c.1760-1802)

Australian Aboriginal History

1788 marked the most dramatic change in Australia's long and ancient history. The English from the First Fleet, which consisted of 11 ships and over 1,400 people, set up their tents in Sydney Cove. Those on the First Fleet were mainly convicts and the British soldiers who guarded them.

Nothing like this had ever happened before for Aboriginal people. These strangers from across the sea were helping themselves to fish from the harbour and sea, and animals and plants from the land.

Captain Arthur Phillip, now Governor of the new colony, claimed New South Wales for the British Crown. Phillip was given authority to take half a continent from the local inhabitants who had been living on the continent for 65,000 years.

Eora

While Aborigines were to be protected under British law this did not mean much for the Eora people (Aborigines living in areas around Sydney) particularly when they saw their lands being devastated: trees cut down, food and tools stolen, bush cleared, roads built, and houses erected.

The Eora people lived in family groups and were connected by common language and kinship. They were hunter-gatherers who lived an affluent way of life enjoying the richness and ready availability of food and water resources of the Sydney coastal region. They must have been shocked and distressed at what they could see happening to their country.

From the beginning the Eora were angered. As Governor Phillip landed in Botany Bay and later at

Port Jackson, the Eora people met him in armed groups. Two convicts were killed because they had stolen tools and offended local Aboriginal laws.

Pemulwuy

From the people around Botany Bay there emerged a powerful guerrilla leader or resistance hero. This was Pemulwuy (c.1760-1802). He was a Bidjigal man from the Botany Bay area of Sydney. The English soon relegated his status to that of outlaw.

Pemulwuy had two distinguishing physical features - a left eye with a speck or brown mark on it, and a club foot, which was the result of an injury.

Pemulwuy was also said to be a "clever man" which is a very special person in traditional Aboriginal society who possessed extraordinary or supernatural powers.

Pemulwuy was linked to the killing of one of Governor Phillip's servants, a gamekeeper called McIntyre, who before he died admitted he had committed a number of offences against the Eora.

As the British grew more established and richer in their new colony and able to satisfactorily provide their own food and supplies, the local Eora people became more desperate and bitter, and felt more under threat.

From this time until his death in 1802, Pemulwuy led the Eora resistance against the British settlement which was continually expanding in the Sydney area and encroaching onto Aboriginal lands.

Pemulwuy and his men attacked these unwelcome intruders – raiding settlements, burning houses, destroying crops, and attacking settlers who wandered away from their home bases. In retaliation Governor Phillip sent out soldiers to arrest him.

Pemulwuy couldn't be found. It was thought that a bushranger known as Black Caesar, who was one of several black prisoners from the First Fleet, had killed him. But no, Pemulwuy survived but was badly wounded.

In 1797 the resistance against the English was so severe that settlers and soldiers did everything they could to bring Pemulwuy down.

Parramatta

In a vicious confrontation at Parramatta, Pemulwuy with his army of warriors, marched into the settlement threatening to spear those who stood in their way. The

British soldiers, the redcoats, opened fire killing five of Pemulwuy's men.

The Eora were forced to retreat under the steady and sustained fire from the redcoats. Pemulwuy was wounded and captured, but within a few weeks he escaped but with a leg iron still in place. Once again he was leading the attacks on the invaders.

A legend developed that Pemulwuy could not be killed and would never be defeated. He had been able to avoid lethal bullets and to survive terrible wounds.

Efforts in 1801 were made by Governor Philip Gidley King to turn the Eora against their leader.

The local Aborigines in the Parramatta, Georges River and Prospect Hill areas were to be driven away and kept from the settlements.

They were told that when Pemulwuy's head was brought into the settlement that friendly relations would be restored. Pemulwuy was an outlaw and a reward was offered for him - dead or alive.

In 1802 Pemulwuy was shot by two settlers who had stalked him. His head was cut from his body and pickled. It was preserved in spirits and sent to Sir Joseph Banks in England to add to his collection and for research. Today the current whereabouts of the head is unknown.

Pemulwuy's assassination brought down a hero who had defied several governors in fierce resistance and who had won the admiration of both white and black. Above all he contained for twelve years the cancer like spread of the British invasion into Eora lands.

Australian Aboriginal History

Sources:

Barlow, Alex and Hill, Marji Heroes Of The Aboriginal Struggle. South Melbourne, Vic., Macmillan, 1987. (Australian Aborigines)

Grassby, Al and Hill, Marji Six Australian Battlefields: The Black Resistance To Invasion And The White Struggle Against Colonial Oppression. North Ryde, NSW , Angus & Robertson, 1988.

Hill, Marji First People Then And Now: Introducing Indigenous Australians. Gold Coast, Qld, The Prison Tree Press, 2017.

National Museum of Australia
http://www.nma.gov.au/online_features/defining_moments/featured/pemulwuy

Chapter 3

Musquito
(c.1780 – 1825)

Australian Aboriginal History

Musquito (c.1780 – 1825) was one of the early resistance fighters on Australia's east coast. He emerged in the Hawkesbury River and Broken Bay regions of New South Wales.

In 1805 Musquito was transported to Norfolk Island most likely for leading the attacks against the British settlers who were invading his country along the lower Hawkesbury River.

Norfolk Island is located approximately 1000 kilometres off the east coast of Australia and at the time of Musquito, it was a penal settlement.

Musquito was possibly a Kuring-gai man from around Broken Bay in New South Wales although the Australian Dictionary of Biography says he was an Eora man, born on the north shore of Port Jackson, New South Wales.

Musquito led many of the raids on settlers and their property along the New South Wales Central coast.

Aboriginal resistance

From Norfolk Island in 1813, Musquito was sent to Launceston in Tasmania, then called Van Diemans Land.

The Lieutenant-Governor at the time, Colonel William Sorell, sought Musquito's help in tracking down bushranger, Michael Howe. Sorrell had been impressed with Musquito's abilities as a tracker, so in return for doing this Musquito was promised his freedom to return to his people in New South Wales.

In 1818 Musquito was put to work as a stockman for one of the British settlers, Edward Lord. In October of that year Musquito succeeded in helping to find the bushranger, Michael Howe, and kill him. However, Sorrell broke his promise of freedom.

In about 1819 Musquito, very antagonistic towards the white settlers, became a bushranger himself and went to the Tasmanian bush and joined the Laremairremener people from Oyster Bay. Joining forces they ran guerrilla campaigns against the British.

Musquito's expertise as a guerrilla resistance fighter, together with his knowledge of English language and English customs, were assets to the local Laremairremener people who wanted to retaliate against the English aggression.

Uniting with "Black Jack" another resistance fighter, Musquito led a series of successful attacks on outlying farms on the east coast of Tasmania in 1823 and in

1824. He is alleged to have participated in offensives which resulted in the death of several colonists.

The military then was on his trail.

Capture

Lieutenant-Governor George Arthur offered a reward for Musquito's capture and he was captured in 1825.

Musquito's several years of successful guerrilla warfare came to an end when two bushrangers-cum-bounty hunters led by a renegade called Teague tracked him down.

A wounded Musquito and his fellow resistance fighter, Black Jack, were taken back to Hobart where they were eventually publicly hanged on 24 February 1825.

At this time in Tasmanian history the extremely violent Black War was at its height. This resulted in the near genocide of the Indigenous population.

It has been suggested by Dr Michael Powell that the hanging of Musquito would have stirred up a ground swell of ill-feeling and well may have contributed to the Black War at the time.

Australian Aboriginal History

Sources:

Australian Dictionary Of Biography
http://adb.anu.edu.au/biography/musquito-13124

Barlow, Alex and Hill, Marji The Macmillan Encyclopedia Australia's Aboriginal Peoples. South Yarra, Vic, Macmillan, 2000.

Grassby, Al and Hill, Marji Six Australian Battlefields. North Ryde, NSW, Angus & Robertson , 1988.

Powell, Michael in http://www.abc.net.au/news/2016-12-02/musquito-and-tasmanias-black-war/8075714

Wise, C. "Black rebel: Mosquito" pp. 1-7 in E.Fry (ed), *Rebels And Radicals*. Sydney, Allen & Unwin, 1983.

Chapter 4

Windradyne
(c.1800–1829)

Windradyne (c.1800–1829), also known as "Saturday," was a resistance fighter and warrior who led the guerrilla resistance against the British invasion of Wiradjuri lands in the Bathurst region of New South Wales in the 1820s.

Lure of the west

After the First Fleet arrived from England in January 1788, the frontier resistance wars that took place on the Australian soil started in Sydney.

As the European population increased in the new colony there was increasing contact between them and the local Eora people. This contact led to conflict and which was to escalate over the next one hundred years.

From this time on from the aggressive conflict between two opposing cultures there emerged a powerful

Aboriginal guerrilla leader. This was Pemulwuy (c.1760-1802).

As British settlement became more established in this new colony and as the settlers were able to satisfactorily provide their own food and supplies, the Eora people became more desperate and bitter, and more under threat.

Pemulwuy led the Eora guerrilla resistance against the British settlement which was continually expanding. Pemulwuy and his men attacked the aliens – raiding settlements, burning houses, destroying crops, and going after colonists who ventured beyond their home boundaries.

The country over and beyond the Blue Mountains remained isolated from the conflict that was taking place in the Sydney region. The Blue Mountains had provided a barrier to this British expansion.

But by 1813 the explorers Gregory Blaxland, William Lawson, and William Wentworth crossed the Blue Mountains and they discovered the rich countryside belonging to the traditional inhabitants, the Wiradjuri people.

Governor Lachlan Macquarie commissioned a road to be built across the mountains which was completed in early 1815.

Wiradjuri Country

Wiradjuri country covered an area larger than England with the first people occupying the central rivers and plains area of New South Wales.

Wiradjuri country covers roughly all the area from Nyngan and Dubbo to Lithgow and Bathurst and south to Albury and west to Hay.

The Wiradjuri nation supported a large population but with the incursion of the British into these lands the Wiradjuri suffered greatly at the hands of these early immigrants.

Like other Indigenous nations the Wiradjuri were divided into clans each belonging to a defined territory. Family groups moved over the lands which containing the food and water supplies and the sacred sites essential to the religious and ceremonial life of the people.

Scattered throughout the length and breadth of Wiradjuri country were bora grounds where large groups would gather for ceremonies. Another cultural feature of the region were the carved tress or dendroglyths which were associated with burial customs.

The designs carved into the trees were also replicated in designs on human bodies and weapons.

Grab for land

British landholders had an insatiable greed for more land and there was unplanned and unregulated occupation of thousands of hectares of Wiradjuri land along the Fish and Macquarie Rivers.

Bathurst became a military and supply base for the British aggressors.

Tensions developed as the red coated soldiers arrived with convicts. At gun point the newcomers took over the best land and the permanent water supplies. This action forced the Wiradjuri from their traditional camp grounds and denied them access to their food and water resources.

The penetration into Wiradjuri lands was fast and at many places along the Wiradjuri open frontier there were fresh intrusions into Wiradjuri country.

The Wiradjuri witnessed the deadly danger of British firearms. They saw soldiers, chain gangs, and great herds of cattle and sheep moving into the places they traditionally occupied.

Traditional food supplies were destroyed. Water supplies were fouled. The British did as they pleased.

Having stolen lands and food resources the intruders turned to the women. Wiradjuri wives and daughters were taken away by force and raped. The Wiradjuri found themselves economically dispossessed overnight.

By 1820 the Wiradjuri were facing a very powerful, British presence in their country. They did not know it, but the odds were being increasingly stacked against them.

The Wiradjuri were ready to fight as already blood had been spilt on their soil in defence of their land and families.

Fighting west of the Blue Mountains had broken out as the British challenged the Wiradjuri nation.

Windradyne, who had emerged as the leader of the Wiradjuri resistance, led raids throughout 1823 and he and his men attacked outlying stations. His raiding parties attacked properties, burnt down buildings, killed garrisons, and destroyed sheep and cattle.

More troops were sent in from Sydney and the 2nd Somersetshire Regiment (40th) moved out from Bathurst to confront Windradyne and his warriors.

Windradyne was so successful in leading his fighters that the British declared Martial Law in 1824.

Windradyne's reputation and standing among his people grew higher than ever. His strength and stamina became legendary.

After the death of two stockmen at Kings Plains, Windradyne was arrested and put into prison. Windradyne was so strong and powerful that the story goes that it took six men and a severe beating to hold him down.

Battle of Bathurst

Battles were fought in and around the Bathurst district. Battles turned into massacres and this policy of massacre included the killing of women and children as well as the warriors.

What has been regarded as the Battle of Bathurst commenced about 10 September 1824 when Windradyne and about thirty warriors set out to clear stock and people from an area on the Cudgegong River. This was around 130 kilometres north of Bathurst.

Fighting broke out between the Wiradjuri and a small group of three English men. Half the Wiradjuri were either killed or wounded.

The British assembled a large infantry and sent them into action. Seventy-five soldiers and one hundred local mounted auxiliaries moved out of Bathurst in the culmination of an extermination war.

On 18 September 1824 for about ten days the British infantry sought out and killed the Wiradjuri, and systematically destroyed everything.

Wiradjuri people were hunted like dogs. They were surrounded and shot. The British campaign was one of extermination.

Daily there were reports of slaughter and the killing fields continued for a couple of months.

A reward of 500 acres (202.3 ha) was offered for Windradyne's capture.

By November small groups of Wiradjuri began to surrender.

Wiradjuri casualties were in the hundreds as the British firepower and tactics caused a devastating toll on the Wiradjuri.

In the long drawn out battle which turned into massacre it is estimated that one-third of the local Wiradjuri population was wiped out.

But the British authorities failed to capture Windradyne and this delayed the repeal of martial law until 11 December. On this day 1824 Governor Brisbane finally lifted martial law formally ending months of hostilities.

Peace

Windradyne and his now small guerrilla force of four to eight men moved through the Bathurst district.

The British had been unable to kill or capture him so the British authorities decided to offer Windradyne peace with honour.

The Governor wanted to meet Windradyne who had defied his soldiers for so long. Windradyne was a man who had become a legend in his own lifetime.

Messages were sent back and forth across the ranges from Sydney to Bathurst, and it was arranged that Windradyne should meet Governor Brisbane in the market place at Parramatta at noon on Tuesday, 28 December 1824.

Windradyne and about 260 of his people - men, women and children - trekked for seventeen days the 200 kilometres across the ranges to Parramatta for a peace conference with Governor Brisbane.

Clad in their long possum skin cloaks Windradyne and his followers were joined by other Wiradjuri clans until there were some 400 Wiradjuri present.

Windradyne had a strong physical presence with an impressive muscular physique and a piercing eye.

The Governor formally proclaimed the lifting of martial law. The war was over and peace would reign.

Windradyne was presented with a straw hat decorated with a label bearing the word "peace" and a little branch representing the olive. Following the proclamation a peace feast began.

This peace conference ended the days when Windradyne would lead his guerrilla forces against the British.

In December 1825 Windradyne was again invited to Parramatta. This time the invitation came from Governor Brisbane's successor, Ralph Darling.

The governor and all the well to do and powerful of the colony eagerly awaited Windradyne's acceptance but they were to be disappointed. Windradyne sent his apologies. He was busy and unable to accept as he was involved in preparing a ceremony with a neighbouring clan.

Windradyne said he would meet the Governor at another time.

He continued to give leadership holding his people together and trying to bind the wounds and the coming to terms with the occupation of their lands.

Death of Windradyne

Wherever Windradyne went he was greeted with affection. An Englishman described him as a "fine figure" and almost Apollo like.

While Windradyne made peace with the British invaders he sometimes had disagreements with his fellow men.

When a Wiradjuri group came to visit him a dispute broke out and Windradyne was wounded in the knee. He ended up in the local hospital where his wound was dressed and he was looked after by some of the convict women.

Hospital was just too much! He tore off his bandages and headed for a Wiradjuri burial ground where his wound turned gangrenous. He died on 21 March,

1829. Windradyne's death has also been recorded as 1835.

Windradyne was given a ceremonial burial wrapped in his possum skin cloak with his weapons bearing his clan designs. His grave was marked by a large mound of timber and earth flanked by two wild apple trees.

He had been closely associated with George Suttor, and his son William Henry, who owned the *Brucedale* property. One hundred and twenty years later the Suttor family erected a memorial over the grave as a tribute to the fallen warrior.

Brucedale was the historic heart of Wiradjuri land in the Bathurst region and was the site of one of their sacred burial grounds.

There are various accounts of Windradyne's death and burial but the Suttor family claimed that Windradyne did leave Bathurst Hospital and went to join his people near *Brucedale* and that he died on the property.

On 25 April 1954 Mrs Roy Suttor unveiled the memorial with a plaque that said:

> Last resting place of Windradyne, alias Saturday
>
> Last chief of the Aborigines.
>
> First a terror but later a friend of the settlers
>
> Died of wounds received in a tribal encounter 1835.
>
> A true patriot.

Sources:

Australian Dictionary Of Biography.
> http://adb.anu.edu.au/biography/windradyne-13251

Barlow, Alex and Hill, Marji The Macmillan Encyclopedia Australia's Aboriginal Peoples. South Yarra, Vic, Macmillan, 2000.

Grassby, Al and Hill, Marji Six Australian Battlefields: The Black Resistance To Invasion And The White Struggle Against Colonial Oppression. North Ryde, NSW , Angus & Robertson, 1988.

Chapter 5

Yagan
(c.1795-1833)

The story of Yagan (c.1795-1833) is about the taking over of Aboriginal lands in Western Australia by the British colonists. Yagan was a hero of the Australian Aboriginal resistance of the Swan River and since his time he has become an iconic figure and symbol of the fight for Nyungar rights and recognition.

Aboriginal people fought wars of resistance against the British Empire starting on the east coast of the Australian continent in 1788 a couple of years after the arrival of the First Fleet.

The Aboriginal people of southwest Western Australia are generally known as Nyungar (Nyoongar, Noongar).

The Nyungar fiercely defended their rights and their lands. Here is their story.

Invasion of the west

The Nyungar owned their country for many thousands of years. While they quietly lived mostly in peace and tranquillity, over in Europe plans were afoot by the Dutch, the English, the French and the Portuguese to explore and take over the western half of Australia.

The ships of the Dutch East India Company were the first to report on the west coast of Australia. These ships were carried there often by accident because of inaccurate navigation aids and the ocean currents.

The first recorded sighting of the west coast was made in 1616 by Dirk Hartog in the *Eendracht*. The *Zeewulf* came unexpectedly to the coast two years later. In 1619 there were another two ships. In 1622 there was the *Leeuwin,* which sighted and named the south west tip of the continent.

In 1644 Abel Tasman charted the north-west coast from Darwin to Dampier. In 1658 Captain Peerebroom on the *Elburgh* recorded observations of the Nyungar people of southwest Australia near Cape Leeuwin.

The voyage of Willem de Vlamingh in 1696-97 was the biggest large-scale effort by the Dutch East India Company to find new worlds in the Australian continent. It also marked the last attempt by the Dutch to penetrate the mysteries of the great southern land.

The British

While the various European empires probed the southern continent they did not establish a permanent presence.

The forerunner of the British takeover of the continent was when a British ship, the *Tryal*, was wrecked off the west coast in 1622. Then in 1688 an English pirate, William Dampier with a group of English buccaneers in a stolen ship, the *Cygnet,* landed near what is now Derby.

Nearly 100 years later in September 1791 Captain George Vancouver in the *Discovery* discovered and named King George Sound. Captain Matthew Flinders commanding the Investigator followed in December 1801.

All was to change for the Nyungar when in 1827 Captain James Stirling came to the Swan River.

The French

The inspiration of Napoleon Bonaparte as Emperor of the French carried the French to the furthest corners of the world. Captain Nicolas Baudin commanding *Le*

Geographe and *La Naturaliste* arrived in Western Australia in 1801. In February 1803 Baudin and his men also established contact with the Nyungar people at King George Sound.

In October 1826, Captain Dumont D'Urville commanding *L'Astrolabe* landed at King George Sound to establish a scientific observatory.

The age old rivalry between England and France flared as soon as the French flag was observed in Australian waters. The British Government and its colonial administration were immediately suspicious that France might claim and colonise that half of the continent not covered by Cook's proclamation of 1770.

Eager to stop any French takeover of the west led to the hurried establishment of British garrisons in northern and southern Australia in the 1820s.

A peace is shattered

Tragically, the peace of the south-west was shattered by gangs of sealers from Bass Strait. They began to raid Nyungar dwellings to kidnap women and female children. The sealers also brought with them infectious diseases to which the Nyungar had no resistance.

Phillip Parker King, Governor of NSW, followed up the visits of Vancouver and Flinders to King George Sound in January 1818.

In 1829 the British Government decided to establish the colony of Western Australia with Captain James Stirling as its Lieutenant-Governor. This was the year all was to change for Aboriginal people of the west.

In March 1827 Stirling arrived at the Swan River. He made his initial contact with the local inhabitants when he proceeded to explore up the river.

He met and interacted with a group of about thirty Nyungar men and they traded spears and woomeras for clothing and swans. The meeting was friendly.

A second major meeting with the Nyungar took place near today's Busselton when Stirling sailed south. Again it was peaceful. A Nyungar senior man gave a sign of peace by leaving his spears behind him. The warrior removed his kangaroo-skin cloak to reveal that no weapons were concealed on his body.

Reports of these early meetings with the Nyungar people greatly impressed Governor Darling. Stirling's success was rewarded with him being given 2,560 acres (1,035.995 hectares) of land in New South Wales near Bathurst . This was the usual practice of colonial governments to give land to their naval captains.

Returning to the Swan River in 1829 Stirling established a settlement and was given the rank and authority of Lieutenant-Governor.

Not only was he given the authority to seize all the land belonging to the people of the west without discussion, treaty or agreement of any kind, he received a personal gift of 100,000 acres (40,468.56 hectares).

The first ship bringing settlers from England to the west was the *Parmelia*. It arrived on 2 June, 1829. Then on 18 June, Stirling proclaimed British rule, with all the people of the west becoming "British subjects of King George IV".

Eighteen ships from the Britain arrived between August and December 1829 to the Swan River so British colonists quickly spread over the land.

Taking the best fertile areas and lands on the river they then set to clear the timber, build homesteads, and to run sheep and cattle over their new lands.

The British were for the most part unaware that all the land, every billabong, creek, river, hill or valley, was the property of the Nyungar people whose religious belief was that the ancestral beings of the Dreamtime had given the land to them to be cared for forever.

The Pemulwuy tradition

When the inevitable conflict broke out with the newcomers, Yagan emerged as a resistance leader in the tradition established by Pemulwuy who led the

Australian Aboriginal History

Eora resistance in the Sydney region in the 1790s against the British.

In Sydney, where the first wars of resistance took place, nothing like this had ever happened before for Australia's first people as these strangers from over the seas were taking fish from the harbour and sea, and animals and plants from the land.

Cook had declared that Australia was *terra nullius* meaning that the Australian continent was uninhabited, unoccupied and unowned. This was the justification that the British used to claim the country as theirs. From this time on the lives of Aboriginal Australians changed forever and being subjected to a foreign power they had no rights of any kind.

Captain Arthur Phillip had claimed New South Wales for the British Crown. The British Government had given him authority to take half a continent from the Aboriginal inhabitants, ignorant of the fact that its first people was one of the earliest centres of civilisation in the world with its history and culture dating as far back as 65,000 years.

From this time until his death in 1802, Pemulwuy led the Eora resistance with guerrilla style tactics against the British settlement which was continually expanding over Aboriginal lands.

A generation later Yagan suffered the same fate of assassination just like Pemulwuy. Yagan's head, also, was hacked from the body and sent to England.

Australian frontier wars were to continue throughout the remaining century.

Australian Aboriginal History

The new colony

The Nyungar name for the new Swan River was Mooro. The site of Perth itself was known as Boorloo.

Yellagonga was the senior man and lawman so he became the representative for the people of that area. His main camp was located on the sloping hill called Byerbup, which gave him an excellent view of the town and the river flats.

In this early phase of settlement the Nyungar were able to maintain their traditional lifestyle. They would trade fish and game for bread and flour and they would move in and out of the town of Perth.

The fact that the Nyungar tolerated the English intruders and maintained peaceful relations was because of Yellagonga's leadership and a belief that these strangers were spirits returned from the dead.

English men and women often found themselves being greeted as returned fathers or mothers, brothers or sisters.

British security in the colony lay with the muskets of the officers and men of the West Suffolk (63rd) Regiment and the arms of the crew and marines from the ships. In addition, almost all the settlers had access to European style weapons.

Within five years the British settlement was nearly 2,000 strong. It consisted mostly of men - soldiers, sailors and landowners.

Once the British were settled on their blocks of land they faced a struggle to survive in a completely alien environment. To put up a house, to grow some food, just to survive in the early days totally pre-occupied them.

But consciously they set out to duplicate their homeland, ripping out local trees and shrubs and substituting roses and oaks. They scattered the region with English names such as Guildford, Bayswater and Huntingdale.

The seeds of war were sown by the different cultural concepts of land and its management.

At the end of the first year of British settlement, the Nyungar began to fire the land. This was an annual practice to encourage growth, hunt out game and increase soil fertility. It is known as "firestick farming".

However, firing the land was a threat to the homesteads of the settlers and to their crops and livestock. The British visitors did as they pleased, taking the traditional game of the Nyungar such as kangaroos and other native game. However, the intruders regarded their own livestock as private property.

The Nyungar, seeing their own livestock being depleted, began to retaliate by taking English poultry, sheep and cattle. Before long the local Indigenous were branded as thieves and rogues.

Within the first year of settlement there were clashes between the opposing cultures. An example of one of these clashes was an incident in the first year of settlement. A group of Nyungar, discovering that their game had gone, turned to some chickens. The Englishman defended his chickens, the military were called, and they fired on the Nyungar to drive them away.

While the English did not shoot to kill, the damage was done. The Nyungar had found a new rule: "We take what you have but you can't take what we have".

Over the next couple of years incidents like this multiplied. Conflict grew. A group of guerrilla resistance leaders emerged: Yagan from the Swan River, Weeip from the Upper Swan River, and Calyute from Pinjarra.

Resistance begins

Nyungar resistance gathered momentum during 1832 and 1833 with isolated farms becoming targets of guerrilla attacks.

English settlers were frightened to wander too far away from their homesteads. Tensions heightened and citizen forces were recruited to assist the military with much of the activity happening on the Swan and Canning Rivers.

Nyungar warriors preferred their traditional weapons. However, this failure to use the new, European firearms made it impossible for the local Nyungar people to withstand frontal attacks from the guns of the enemy.

The Nyungar used glass chips instead of stone flakes on their spears and substituted metal axes for stone. They were armed with spear throwers or woomeras, spears, axes, shields, boomerangs and throwing sticks.

A spear point was edged with razor-sharp quartz or glass flakes embedded in hardened tree gum. As it passed through an enemy's flesh the quartz edges severed the blood vessels. When it was withdrawn pieces of quartz would break off and remain inside the victim. This spear was designed to inflict maximum damage. It was propelled by a woomera, which increased its range, speed and accuracy. Shields were used for protection in action, but were designed to deflect spears not bullets.

As Nyungar resistance gathered momentum the British demanded military action.

On 14 June 1832 a group of Nyungar speared a bullock belonging to one of the settlers. Here was another instance of the Nyungar finding their traditional food having been replaced by cattle.

The reaction was a raid by ten armed Englishmen on a camp of fifty men, women and children. Each side had deaths and the Nyungar camp surrendered. The surviving Nyungar men, women and children were herded together and were given a severe warning not to touch the sacred English cows again.

Fear of a mass attack on Perth grew. Food depots were established outside Perth and Fremantle in an effort to prevent the Nyungar from moving around the settlements. Troops were placed strategically to provide early warning should large numbers of warriors attempt to cross the Swan River by way of the swamp flats.

Some Englishmen spoke out in concern about what was happening to the Nyungar. One outspoken settler was Robert Menli Lyon. He condemned the actions of the British against the Nyungar and he pointed out that the British were seizing land that was not theirs.

> "You have seized upon a land that is not yours. Beware, and do not as a people, add to this guilt

of dipping your hands in the blood of those whom you have spoiled of their country." (Perth Gazette, 9 March 1933)

Yagan the leader

Yagan was gaining prominence as a resistance leader in the region.

Like many outstanding personalities there was a dualism in his character. While Yagan could be gentle he could also be very fierce. The Late Ken Colbung (Nundjan Djiridjarkan) (1931-2010), an elder and a descendent of Yagan, believed that in Yagan's dealings with the English he could share game and be friendly, but given his sense of justice he was quick to balance the scales and could become a formidable foe.

It was not obvious whether Yagan had a wife or children. When he was killed he was survived by his mother, Moyran and two brothers. Just like other men of his culture, Yagan hunted played, danced, loved and lived. It is estimated that he was close to 40 years of age when he died.

Advocate for peace

When the British first met Yagan they liked and respected him. He was described as a "true prince of his people" and was tall, intelligent, swaggering.

Before the outbreak of fighting, between his people and the British, Yagan was a favourite of the English. He would play with them; carry their children on his shoulders; have fun with them.

He would perform the ceremonial dances of his people in front of the Governor. The English described him performing with "infinite dignity and grace".

Yagan was an advocate for peace between the Nyungar and the British.

Outlaw

But conflict between the British settlers and the Nyungar kept surfacing. Each incident inflamed passions, regardless of where the guilt lay.

The killing of the Velvick brothers near Fremantle turned them into pioneer martyrs. The Velvick brothers were an unpleasant duo. They had already been convicted and punished by their own people for mercilessly beating Nyungar men and women.

They murdered the brother of Yagan. This was Domjum. A group of Yagan's people, including Domjum, broke into a store on the night of 29 April 1833 to take some flour. They thought that no one was there, but the owner was in the store. The Nyungar party was fired upon and two were killed. Domjum was one of them and his head was hacked from his body.

Yagan and his father, Midgigooroo had to avenge the death. They had to carry out traditional law. It was their job to seek retribution for the two deaths through the system of payback.

A Mr Phillips believed that he saw Yagan spearing the body of one of the deceased. Yagan's men (about 50 of them) were identified including his father, Midgigooroo.

Yagan evaded capture but his father, Midgigooroo, was caught by British soldiers. He was sent to gaol and two days later, Midgigooroo was executed.

A Proclamation was issued which offered a reward for Yagan – alive or dead.

Yagan's fate

The fate of Yagan in Western Australia in the early 1800s was death at the hands of the British. He was lured into an ambush, shot, his head severed, his entire skin cut off and the head smoked to preserve it.

Yagan's hair was combed, possum fur string was tied around the head as a headband, and red and black cockatoo features were added.

The head was sent to England as a souvenir.

In 1964 the head was buried in a Liverpool cemetery. Efforts by Australians to bring Yagan's head home culminated in 1997 when a four person delegation led by West Australian Aboriginal elder, Ken Colbung, went to England to negotiate its return.

The intervention of the British Prime Minister, Tony Blair, and members of the British Parliament enabled justice to be done and arrangements were made for Yagan's head to be returned to Western Australia.

On the 1 September 1997, a delegation of Elders brought Yagan's head back to his home country.

The reburial of his remains took place in a ceremony on the 10 July 2010.

The life and struggles of Yagan can be summed up in his own words:

Australian Aboriginal History

You came to our own country… you have driven us from our haunts and disturbed us in our occupation as we walk in our own country… we are fired upon by white men, why should they mistreat us this way?

(Yagan, 1832)

Sources:

Colbung, Ken Yagan: the Swan River Settlement. Australia Council for the Arts.

Durack, Mary Yagan of the Bibbulman. West Melbourne, Nelson, 1976.

Grassby, Al & Hill, Marji Six Australian Battlefields. Sydney, Allen & Unwin, 1998.

Green, Neville Broken Spears. Perth, Focus Education Services, 1984.

Green, Neville, ed. Nyungar: the People: Aboriginal Customs in the Southwest of Australia. Creative Research Perth and Mt Lawley College 1979.

Koori Mail.

Reuter Information Service.

Nando Times News.

The West Australian. Tues. April 12, 1994.

https://www.noongarculture.org.au/yagan/

http://www.nma.gov.au/exhibitions/first_australians/resistance/yagan/finding_yagan

Chapter 6

Jandamarra
(c.1873-1897)

Australian Aboriginal History

Jandamarra (c.1873-1897) was a hero of the Aboriginal resistance in the Kimberley region of Western Australia in the 1890s. He is famous for the successful resistance campaigns that took place at Windjina Gorge in 1894 and 1895.

Jandamarra led organised guerrilla insurrections against British pastoralists who were overrunning Bunuba lands. For over three years Jandamarra, armed with his intimate knowledge of Bunuba country together with his understanding of the ways of the British, protected his people and country against the intruders who were occupying his lands and destroying the traditional economy.

Jandamarra, also known as Pigeon, was a Bunuba man from the West Kimberley.

Bunuba country

Bunuba country is situated in the Kimberleys in the far north of Western Australia. It extended from Fitzroy Crossing to the King Leopold Ranges and included the Napier and Oscar Ranges.

The stunning Windjina Gorge with its majestic, water-streaked cliffs is located in Bunuba country. The name Windjina, was mis-recorded by the English pastoralist who built *Lillimooloora* homestead in 1884.

Windjina Gorge, which cuts through the Napier Range, is where Jandamarra had his hideout when he led the resistance against the British invasion of his lands in 1894.

During the wet season in northern Australia, which are those few months between October and April, warm, moist and monsoonal northwest winds bring high humidity and heavy rainfall.

This is when the Lennard River is full of water and flows through the Windjina Gorge.

During the dry season, however, which is between May and September, dry southeast winds bring about low humidity and low rainfall. All the waterholes and creeks become dry.

The Lennard River dries up and leaves pools of water surrounded by trees and bush - a haven for crocodiles and flying foxes (fruit bats).

Wandjina spirit figures

Windjina Gorge for Bunuba people is a very spiritual place because this is where the very powerful

Wandjina creation spirits live. Rock art in the Kimberley region in northwest of Western Australia is well known for its Wandjina spirit figure images.

Wandjinas are huge spirit beings, almost human in form, with large headdresses. The Wandjinas are believed to be the clouds which form before the rains begin because it is believed they are responsible for bringing the rains.

They are powerful spirit beings. Wandjinas are so powerful that people today still take great care when approaching a Wandjina site. They call out to the spirit beings to let them know that they are approaching and to assure the Wandjinas that they will do no harm to their images on the rock walls.

Stockman

Jandamarra was just a small boy when the first of the British colonists started invading Bunuba lands. Conflict with these unwelcome pastoralists who were occupying traditional country and who were driving sheep and cattle into the region had already started.

Jandamarra at the age of eleven went to live in his mother's country on the Lennard River. This area had become a cattle property run by William Lukin. Very soon Lukin discovered that Jandamarra had many talents and abilities.

As a teenager, Jandamarra got a reputation for his abilities as a stockman and shearer. Lukin named him "Pigeon" because he was a small man but very fast on his feet. He also had a cheeky personality.

Among his own people Jandamarra was regarded as an excellent hunter. He emerged as a leader and started attacking the white frontier.

In 1889 on the Lennard River and at *Lillimooloora*, resistance fighters slaughtered several thousand sheep. All of these attacks were led by Jandamarra.

Resistance fighting

The British invaders reinforced troops in the region and established a military post near Windjina Gorge.

Police troopers captured Jandamarra and fellow resistance fighter, his uncle, Ellemarra.

Ellemarra had been arrested for stock killing in 1886. He ended in up in Roeburn Prison but escaped and walked back 960 kilometres to the Napier Ranges.

Jandamarra and Ellemarra were chained and had to march to Derby. Ellemarra was returned to gaol and the chain gangs and Jandamarra was put to work looking after the police horses where he spent a year. While Jandamarra was at Derby he won popularity and trust. After his release Jandamarra returned to work on *Lennard River Station*.

Sometime later he went to his mountain home where it was alleged that he violated Bunuba law. He found himself in trouble with his elders because he had disregarded traditional kinship law by having involvements with various women.

He fled to another property - *Brooking Springs Station* - where he was indentured for two years.

Jandamarra had a ruthless boss so he ran away. He was then captured and charged for escaping his bondage. His sentence was to serve as a police tracker north of Derby.

The British authorities wanted to use Jandamarra against his own people so Jandamarra helped to locate and capture sixteen Bunuba warriors.

He had formed a close association with Bill Richardson, a stockman. In 1894 Richardson joined the police force and Jandamarra was recruited as a tracker. With another Aboriginal man called "Captain", he was assigned to Constable Richardson.

He once saved Richardson's life during an attack by the Bunuba people.

In this raid the Bunuba resistance fighters were captured and marched to Lillimooloora, 113 kilometres from Derby. *Lillimooloora* homestead had been taken over by the police as an outpost.

Jandamarra was related to all the sixteen Bunuba warriors.

He was informed that while he was away the British had invaded the Bunuba lands and a police trooper at Fitzroy Crossing had been killing his people indiscriminately.

Jandamarra was under pressure from his people to be loyal to his kin and was told by them that his obligations lay with them. Otherwise he would be ostracised by his people.

With his obligation hanging over him and in a dramatic defection, Jandamarra shot Richardson while he slept and released the Bunuba prisoners. One of these was Ellemarra. This action served to restore Jandamarra's place in his own society.

Jandamarra had become very familiar with British fighting tactics. He knew how to handle firearms. He was regarded as a leader and even Ellemarra served under him.

Jandamarra knew that if he was to be successful at waging war against the British he had to acquire firearms.

Jandamarra planned a Bunuba uprising in defence of his country by using firearms and guerrilla tactics. He attacked a delivery wagon and collected guns, ammunition and rations, the resources needed for his campaign. He then trained his men to use these weapons and ammunition.

His plan was to ambush the patrol of police reinforcements and lead his group of newly trained guerrilla fighters down the Lennard River to clear out the British invaders.

The British started to panic and the police were given sweeping powers to put down the Aboriginal resistance fighters.

Battle of Windjina Gorge

The British regarded Jandamarra and Ellemarra as outlaws. Near the entrance to Windjina Gorge, the outlaws launched their first attack and killed two white men.

It was the first time the Bunuba had used guns against British in the Kimberley and it was big news in the press across the west.

The colonists demanded vengeance.

A British officer, Sub-Inspector Drewry, assembled his troopers together and commissioned fifteen hired hands. He then had six Indigenous stockmen from Queensland join Jandamarra pretending that they were his followers.

But Jandamarra and Ellemarra did not trust them. While Ellemarra wanted to kill them, Jandamarra disagreed because he said his argument was with the British not with the Aboriginal people.

This turned out to be a terrible mistake because the Queensland mob informed the British of Jandamarra's whereabouts and his forces.

On 16 November 1895 the Battle of Windjina Gorge commenced.

The British force of thirty men divided into smaller groups of ten and they prepared to ambush

Jandamarra. They moved into the Gorge from three directions.

Jandamarra was wounded but he put up a hard fight. Fighting alongside Jandamarra were some Bunuba women helping to load and reload the guns. They also cared for him while he recovered from his injuries. But Jandamarra's force were defeated and Ellemarra was among the wounded and died from his injuries.

With the help of his female friends who had always been among his followers, Jandamarra hid in a cave. He had managed to escape to his hiding place through an intricate network of caves.

For four months the British attacked the Bunuba and eventually the Bunuba could no longer carry on their resistance.

Jandamarra's hiding place was in his Tunnel Creek Cave, forty-eight kilometres south of Windjina, where he stayed for two years recuperating from injuries. Periodically, he would emerge from hiding to continue the resistance fighting using his guerrilla tactics.

The British pastoralists and police retaliated and massacred many Aboriginal people.

In an effort to free Bunuba prisoners who were marched in chains to gaol Jandamarra was wounded once again but eventually recovered.

He raided *Lillimooloora Station*.

Jandamarra stood on a hill with his men and mocked Sub-Inspector Ord, the successor to Drewry. Ord was of the opinion that Jandamarra would defy the whole of the British army and even enjoy it.

In 1897 sad losses were to unfold. Ellemarra and one of his comrades were captured by the British. They were hanged in Derby.

While the white men tried to hunt down Jandamarra, he always managed to outwit them. His special powers became legendary, for it seemed Jandamarra possessed the special powers of a "clever man" - a man of high degree. He could simply disappear and reappear at will; he could strike and then melt away into the stronghold of the Australian bush.

Jandamarra's response was further attacks but the one at Oscar Range Station was a failure and he retreated to his hideaway in the Tunnel Creek Cave.

Jandamarra's energy had slowed down because of his battle wounds. His demise came when a black tracker, called Micki, found and killed him at Pigeon's Rock not far from his hideout.

The resistance war in the region died with Jandamarra. Guerrilla resistance was at an end.

But going into the new century there were further punitive expeditions and there were calculated attempts at extermination.

In 1922 there was a massacre at the Durack River. Another one took place in the East Kimberleys in 1926.

This era marked the end of the killing fields for Western Australia.

Sources:

Grassby, Al & Hill, Marji Six Australian Battlefields. Sydney, Allen & Unwin, 1998.

Pedersen, Howard "Pigeon: an Australian Aboriginal rebel" pp.7-15 in Bob Reece and Tom Stannage (eds), *European-Aboriginal Relations In Western Australian History*. Nedlands, WA, University of Western Australia Press, 1984.

https://en.wikipedia.org/wiki/Jandamarra

http://ia.anu.edu.au/biography/jandamarra-8822

http://www.jandamarra.com.au/jandamarratheman.html

https://www.kimberleyaustralia.com/story-of-jandamarra.html

https://aiatsis.gov.au/explore/articles/jandamarra-bunuba-warrior

https://www.allenandunwin.com/browse/books/childrens/picture-books/Jandamarra-Mark-Greenwood-illustrated-by-Terry-Denton-9781742375700

http://www.nma.gov.au/kspace/teachers/kimberley/learning/jandamarra

https://www.kimberleyaustralia.com/story-of-jandamarra.html

https://parks.dpaw.wa.gov.au/park/windjana-gorge

Australian Aboriginal History

About Marji Hill

Author & Artist

Throughout her professional life, Marji Hill has been writing books to promote understanding between Aboriginal and Non-Aboriginal Australians. She fostered the spirit of Reconciliation in all her work since she was Research Fellow in Education at the Australian Institute of Aboriginal and Torres Strait Islander Studies (AIATSIS) in Canberra.

From 2008 to 2011, Marji was Deputy Chairperson of the Mosman Branch of Reconciliation Australia.

After starting at AIATSIS in 1976 Marji, together with her late partner, Alex Barlow, produced more than sixty books on all aspects of Aboriginal Australia including the critical, annotated bibliography *Black Australia*.

In 1989 Marji was the Project co-ordinator and one of the researchers and writers of *Australian Aboriginal Culture* the official Australian Government publication on Aboriginal Australians and Torres Strait Islanders. In 1988 her work of non-fiction *Six Australian Battlefields*, which she co-authored with Al Grassby, was published by Angus and Robertson. A decade later it was re-published by Allen & Unwin as a paperback edition.

The 9-volume encyclopaedia *Macmillan Encyclopaedia of Australia's Aboriginal Peoples* was published in 2000 and in 2009 she published *The Apology: Saying Sorry To The*

Stolen Generations. In 2017 Marji published *First People Then And Now: Introducing Indigenous Australians* and in 2021 she published its second edition.

Marji has a Master of Arts specialising in Anthropology from the Australian National University.

Marji is also a professional artist. One of her large oil paintings was included in the 2004-2005 Ballarat Fine Art Gallery Travelling Exhibition *Eureka Revisited: the Contest of Memories*. This exhibition travelled to Melbourne, Canberra and Ballarat - part of the 150 year celebration of the Eureka Stockade.

Another of her paintings hung for many years in the foyer of Jupiter's Casino in Townsville while her portrait of Jupiter Mosman hangs in the World Centre at Charters Towers in North Queensland. These two paintings celebrate the story of Aboriginal boy, Jupiter Mosman who discovered gold at Charters Towers in 1871.

Marji's paintings are held in many private collections in Australia and overseas. She is represented in collections at Ballarat Fine Art Gallery and the Catholic University.

As part of her professional work, Marji has travelled extensively throughout Aboriginal Australia and the Torres Strait.

More Books by Marji Hill

Self-improvement:

Hill, Marji (2014) *Staying Young Growing Old.* Broadbeach, Qld, The Prison Tree Press. https://amzn.to/38R2XNK

Hill, Marji (2020) *How Big Is Your Why? An Author's Guide to Time Management and Productivity to Achieve Transformational Results.* Broadbeach, Qld, The Prison Tree Press. https://amzn.to/3ttxeKk

Hill, Marji (2020) *A Create and Publish Toolbox: 101 Prompts In A Guided Journal To Help You Write, Self-publish, And Market Your Book On Amazon.*

Broadbeach, Qld, The Prison Tree Press.

https://amzn.to/3vzTzHW

Aboriginal Australia:

Hill, Marji (2021) *First People Then And Now: Introducing Indigenous Australians*. 2nd ed. Broadbeach, Qld, The Prison Tree Press.

https://amzn.to/3tnb64P

www.ingramcontent.com/pod-product-compliance
Lightning Source LLC
Chambersburg PA
CBHW051550010526
44118CB00022B/2647